Manifesting Abundance

The Secret to Using the Power of the Mind to Attract the Magic of the Universe to Manifest Prosperity on Every Side of Life: Money, Love, Friendship, Success, Health, Peace and Inner Happiness

Table of Contents

Introduction

The truth of a long-held claim that our thoughts contain pulses of energy has recently been proven to be scientifically true by quantum physics. This just goes to prove that the brain is a more powerful organ than many of us believed. Through manifestation, the thoughts we entertain have a direct impact on the way we live. This means that we can attract into our lives the things we desire the most, but it also serves as a warning to watch our thoughts at all times. It is the thing we focus on, not the thing we desire, that manifests most of the time. So whether you fear something or you desire it, you can expect it to show up in your life sooner or later.

The power of the mind is such that we can only change the external by first changing the internal (i.e. the way we think). When you try to work on external conditions without first finding out what internal circuitry is causing them and fixing those first, your efforts will almost assuredly be in vain. If you can train your mind to only entertain positive thoughts featuring prosperity, health, happiness, and success, you will be on your way to manifesting these very things in your life.

This is what is commonly referred to as 'mind over matter': the concept that you can overcome physical challenges through sheer willpower. It is something that has been used by monks for thousands of years to perform incredible feats of power, including controlling the elements. With enough focus, you also can harness the power of the mind to attract prosperity and success in every area of your life.

All the power of the mind and energy released by our thoughts exists in the universe and is available for anyone to harness. This is the basic definition of the magic of the universe; the belief that your thoughts manifest into reality. The magic of the universe is governed by the law of attraction and other universal laws, including the law of vibration, polarity, and cause and effect among others. By harnessing the magic of the universe through the power of our minds, we can manifest anything we want in our lives, including money, love, friendships, success, health, peace, and inner happiness. If you can manage to manifest excellence in all these areas of your life, then you will have succeeded in attaining the perfect life.

The magic of the universe is a concept that is believed by pretty much all spiritual groups. Some, if not most of them, hold the belief that we can only reach it after death as a reward for good behavior on earth. We are all spirits, and we are linked to the universe through energy that our spirits release. But here is the main point about the magic of the universe; it only works if you believe in it and actively try to activate it in your own life.

Chapter 1: Manifesting

When it comes to manifesting, the first rule is that you can only manifest those things that you believe are possible. Essentially, whatever you hold to be possible deep down is what you will make come true. The second rule is that your mind must be in the right place. In this chapter, we will look at the first rule by discussing the magic of the universe and the second one by examining the superconscious.

The Magic of the Universe

One thing that scientists and spiritualists agree is the fact that the universe is bigger than is possible to measure, catalogue, or explore. It has infinite dimensions and limitless power that scientific inquiry probably never will uncover. And it is in this mystery and awe that we find the magic of the universe.

First off, the magic of the universe allows us to create our own luck in life. This is an idea whose foundation can be found in the basic beliefs about the universe; it is probabilistic, not deterministic. In a deterministic universe, everything is set in stone while a probabilistic universe gives rise to a world where you can do anything as long as you put your mind to it. It is the spring from which all hope flows, the assurance that the more you do something, the more you move the odds in your favor, and the more likely you are to get a favorable outcome.

Second, the magic of the universe is such that we can make incredible things happen by invoking universal power. Think of it like spell magic but instead of saying a word and waving a wand to make things happen, you think it, work for it, and, ultimately, get it. Now I'm not saying that it's not a lot of work manifesting the magic of the universe in your life- quite the opposite, actually. Within the law of physics, you can work towards anything you want.

So don't think that you can manifest money out of nowhere and do it with enough frequency or in enough quantities to grow rich and successful. That is beyond the reach of the universe and even if you do it once or twice, the odds are against you to a large extent. The magic of the universe will help you get your dream job, meet the love of your life, or attain a perfectly peaceful life, but if you don't take the steps necessary to get there, you will end up stuck in place, unable to move forward.

A belief in the magical universe helps us shift our mind from short to long term thinking. The only thing we can be absolutely sure about is today. What we do right now also reverberates into the future and affects everything in our lives going forward. So, when you start believing in the magic of the universe, you visualize a better tomorrow. Taking it further, you begin to see the merit in taking time out of your day to work towards that vision.

A belief in the magic universe also helps us overcome our fears. You recognize that nothing could go wrong, but if it were to go wrong, you'd be equipped to deal with any difficulties that arise. Because our minds are receptors of the best capacity, we can invite this magic of the universe to manifest in our own lives. And that is the basis of manifestation. We know we can manifest because we believe in a magic universe in which prosperity can be attained through the power of the mind.

The Superconscious

The human mind comprises of three levels of awareness: the conscious, subconscious, and superconscious. All three levels of awareness serve a specific role in our lives. The conscious is the way we see the world. It comprises of the five common senses. Below that is the subconscious, a level of awareness comprising of previous experiences that determines the way we think, act, and feel in every situation. These two levels of awareness are comparatively easy to log onto, but they can only take you so far. Their reach into the universe, while substantial, is woefully limited to the things of the universe that can be perceived in the physical world. However, the universe is like an iceberg which has a lot more of its mass submerged. To reach the deepest parts of the universe and tap into that energy, you are going to have to activate the superconscious.

The superconscious mind is that part of human consciousness that stretches infinitely through space and gives us infinite possibilities for life. It is the part of the mind that is an extension of the magic universe itself. When you get in touch with the superconscious, you recognize not just the infinity of the universe, but also the magic inherent in it. In the superconscious mind, we realize that perfection exists. Every action is inspired by the divine to reverberate through the universe and give you exactly what you need. The superconscious is the part where your mind, heart, and soul interact with the divine.

Simply defined, the superconscious mind is a state of awareness encompassing reality as well as the consciousness and energy behind it. It is a level up from the subconscious and can only be truly experienced through meditation. Its experience is variously described as immense, all-encompassing calm devoid of noise and shadows as might be experienced with the subconscious. Other words to describe the superconscious include peace, tranquility, immense joy, and divine love. When you get to experience superconsciousness, you will have a truly profound spiritual experience and if you are so inclined, ideas for outstanding artwork, poetry, prose, groundbreaking discoveries and innovations, even music will appear.

And the superconscious is also responsible for the universality of thoughts. You see, all thoughts exist in the universal oneness and may be accessed by anyone whose mind is tuned to a particular frequency and is able to reach the level of consciousness in which an idea or thought exists. You may have experienced this when you think about something like a revolutionary new product without knowing it exists only to read somewhere that it is being developed. "An idea whose time has come" is an expression that captured this universality of thoughts quite succinctly. Even in the early civilizations when thoughts and ideas could not travel from one corner of the world to another fast enough, similar innovations often developed in far flung parts of the world.

This is because the superconscious is also known as the "source of infinite wisdom," the "one mind," the "universal mind," among other definitions. All the greatest thinkers were able to come by their groundbreaking ideas by connecting to the superconscious. That is why Socrates' ideas about the mind and Albert Einstein's theories of the world have only been proven true by the passage of time even when many of the older ideas of the universe were disproved. These people were able to connect with the superconscious and draw from the infinite wisdom of the universe.

To manifest prosperity, all three parts of the mind must be aligned. So in the quest to reconnect with the superconscious mind, the subconscious must also come into play. Even though the dreams you have for your life exist in the conscious mind, you can't bypass the subconscious mind. The infinite wisdom moves downwards from the superconscious into the subconscious and then down into the conscious mind for expression. Similarly, in manifesting, you can only receive things in the physical (conscious) after accessing the universe's "Infinite Source" with the subconscious as the link. As soon as you start receiving wisdom from the superconscious, the universe will line everything up so that you can receive everything that you need.

Some of the benefits that you can accrue by accessing the superconscious mind include:

Discovering Your Life's Purpose

Discovering your purpose for living is one of the most rewarding things you can receive in life. A destiny means that you know exactly where to place your energies every day of your life, meaning that you can achieve more and live a more fulfilled life. Every one of us has within their reach a bottomless well of energy that needs only be directed to achieving a superior purpose. When you have nowhere to direct your energy, you will end up wasting it with needless activities.

Now, how exactly do you realize your purpose in life? Because discovering your purpose is the only way to ensure that you don't waste your life. The earlier you discover your purpose, the more time you will have to pull it off. When you tap into the superconscious, you will achieve a profound connection between mind, body, and soul. This enables you to realize your life's mission, access your energy force, harness your talents, and channel them towards a purpose way above yourself.

Develop Empathy

Tapping into the superconscious will enhance the sixth sense provided by the subconscious to give you unparalleled levels of emotional intelligence. It starts by understanding the self: What makes you happy? What drives you crazy? When you start taking note of these things, you also start to see the things that make other people react the same way. You also understand yourself and other people, so you know that all people don't react the same way to the same things. You realize that just because you can't relate to someone's plight from memory (subconscious) does not make it any less distressing. With your newfound super intelligence, you will improve your socialization skills and attract the kind of friends or love interests that you desire. You will also be a better friend and/or lover to the people in your life by understanding them better, even if it is only in an abstract way.

Tapping into the Superconscious

The most successful way to tap into the superconscious mind is by meditating. This allows you to activate the subconscious and, through it, the universal mind. While meditating the superconscious can focus on getting into the alpha state, that blissful sensation of being one with the universe and feeling its power course through your own spirit. If you have already realized your purpose in life, this forms a crucial part of your alpha state through which you can make your way to the superconscious. Obviously, the more you tap into the superconsciousness, the easier it becomes to access it subsequently.

Consciousness Exercises

The conscious mind can be used in manifestation through a very specific process called conscious manifestation. Through conscious manifestation, we aim to create the things we desire by willing them into being. Many people feel helpless when they think about a manifestation exercise in which they have no role or assurance that their desires will be realized. Conscious manifestation effectively takes care of that.

To prepare the mind for conscious manifestation, we must first harness the consciousness of our minds. We must get as close to the superconscious as we can. By doing so, you will develop your capacity to gain new insights about old things by changing your perspective. Tapping into the superconscious also enables you to tap into the universal mind and infinite source so that you can manifest abundance in all areas of your life. Because all the achievements discussed in this book draw from the same infinite source, the process of attaining consciousness in preparation for manifesting them into your life is the same. It follows the steps discussed below.

Quiet the Mind

Even though the mind is made up of three parts: the conscious, subconscious, and superconscious, you can only experience two of them in that order. Consciousness may be experienced with the subconscious (even though you don't pay attention, you can still feel the sensations of the conscious like smell, touch, sound, etc.). In the same way, you can only reach the superconscious by first getting into the subconscious. So, the first process in tuning into the superconscious is turning off the conscious. You can do this through meditation, nature walks, physical exercise, or yoga. Any activity that completely quiets the voice inside your head is an activity that can be a good first step in the journey to achieving superconsciousness.

Tune In

At the same time when the noise inside your mind is diminishing, your ability to listen to your heart increases. The more you quiet the mind, the easier it will become for you to tune into the heart center; a place where compassion, kindness, and love bubble through. You should also pay attention to the deepest parts of your mind. If you are jogging, you can start by zooming in on the vibrations of your feet as they hit the tarmac. If you are tapping into the superconscious through meditation, feel the vibrations of the air as it gets into your body and washes through you. Visualize the whole universe and your position in it. What you are is a speck of energy that is interlinked with every terrestrial and extraterrestrial body. Feel the immensity of the world, the infinite reaches, and the endless energy.

Notice the Synchronicities

The whole idea behind tapping into the superconscious is to synchronize your own energy with the energy of the universe. Now, when you started jogging, or meditating, you took your mind from the conscious into the subconscious; a place where awareness is muted. Now start to increase your awareness of electromagnetic fields in the new zone of consciousness. This consciousness within unconsciousness is what gives the superconscious its immense power. It helps you to attain a level of awareness that is at the same level as the very universe, which is pretty damn high.

The "Consciousness of Poverty"

The consciousness of poverty is a belief that many people have whereby they think that they don't have what it takes to thrive. People with a poverty consciousness look at the world and see an unfriendly place with no compassion for them or their needs. Therefore, there is no use in even dreaming about or hoping for something because it is too big. People who have a poverty consciousness tend to have difficulty appreciating the things they have. Instead of practicing gratitude, they attract lack by their thoughts.

The consciousness of poverty is also manifested through toxic money beliefs. When you think about money and see only the worst things that have been done using money, you condemn yourself to poverty. At best, you can reach the level of sufficient provision, but you will never have enough to meet all your needs. Note very carefully that poverty consciousness is not limited to monetary affairs only. It affects all areas of life, from relationships, health, personal happiness, and fulfillment.

In relationships, poverty consciousness manifests in people who go around thinking that they will never find love. The limiting personal beliefs that these people hold make them feel unwanted and undeserving of love. Until these negative beliefs are eliminated, it is very difficult to find and accept love. The same happens in health, whereby people who expect to stay unhealthy end up suffering bad health. In happiness, as in personal fulfillment, you will never experience these positive emotions until you let yourself. If you believe that you deserve to feel happy, you can and most probably will. If you expect to feel happy after reaching a milestone, you will keep delaying happiness further into the future to infinity.

In this section, we are going to focus on the different ways that you can overcome the consciousness of poverty and manifest abundance in every area of your life.

The first strategy to overcome poverty consciousness is gratitude. Sometimes the reason why we think we are unworthy of riches and prosperity is because we don't recognize just how blessed we are to be where we are today. When you practice gratitude, you remove the focus from your perceived failings and shortcomings and look instead at the positive things that have happened to you for which you can show appreciation.

There are many ways to show gratitude. One way to achieve this is by making a list of ten things for which you are thankful every morning. This way, you start your day with gratitude – a positive, energy-inducing activity that ensures that your whole day is successful and fulfilling as well. Another way is to start a gratitude journal which you can write in throughout the day or fill out in the evening. With a gratitude journal, you focus on the positive things of the day and let them fill your mind. When your conscious mind switches off in sleep and you disappear into the subconscious, you spread the gratitude there as well and attract even more goodness.

The second way to achieve a prosperity consciousness is to live in the moment. A common way that people attract poverty consciousness is by focusing on previous losses instead of current blessings or the promise of the future. Instead of looking to the future to enjoy life, find the things to celebrate about life today. If you can't find that much to be grateful for (and it is entirely possible to have an objectively small number of things for which to be grateful), focus on making the perfect future today. You see, today is the yesterday that the future is born of. Take maximum advantage of the present moment to achieve prosperity tomorrow.

The third way to eliminate the consciousness of poverty is to accomplish something worthwhile. Whether you are feeling overwhelmed by your current sorry state because it is objectively bad or you are simply looking at it the wrong way, you can only turn the situation around by giving your mind something to be grateful for. Focus all your energy on reaching your goals. This way, you will have little time to think about things like whether or not you have what it takes. Before you know it, you will be comfortable aiming for big things because you would have proven yourself capable.

Manifestation

Now let's turn our minds into practical manifestation. According to the law of attraction, it is the process through which we can attract the things we desire into our lives. In manifestation, the thoughts you have play a huge part. In this section, therefore, we will come up with exact thoughts that will put your mind in the right place to manifest your desires from the universe. The following 35 thoughts will help keep you energized, grateful, focused, and excited for the most effective manifestation experience:

Energized

1. I am gaining immense energy and strength even as I eat this food.

Sometimes you eat while doing other things and don't even taste the food, let alone give thought to the reasons why we are eating. This thought reminds you why you are eating and is reinforced by the concrete reminder of food filling your stomach.

2. It is a good time to wake up and get out and about.

When the temptation to snooze that alarm comes, this is the thought that should run through your mind instead.

3. I can ignore my cravings for an extra helping.

As important as it is to remain well fed and full of energy, giving in to cravings for more can backfire badly. When you eat too much, you give your body so much time to digest the food that it has little energy to do anything else. You might have noticed this especially after a heavy lunch. Not to forget that eating too much could make you get even fatter and bring about other health issues like diabetes.

4. Exercise is good for me.

In the morning and throughout the day, exercise keeps your body feeling energetic, refreshes your mind, and makes you perform better.

5. My body is wide awake and my mind is extra-sharp today.
6. I can (and will) take on this day like a boss!
7. My outlook on life is positive and nothing can shake me down.
8. I am blazing with energy right about now!
9. I am beautiful/handsome and strong.
10. My courage and confidence is bubbling over and paving the way for me.
11. Someone really capable has my back – me!
12. I am one with the universe; the universe flows through me.

Gratitude

13. I am truly grateful to the universe for filling my heart and my mind with the right energy to attract abundance.
14. I am enriched from all energy around me.
15. Even this hurdle is teaching me something important and

helping me get to my magical destiny.

16. I am glad to be one of the few to realize the power of the universe.

17. I am grateful for my coworkers who help me become a better employee every day.

18. I am grateful for my customers. My business would be nothing without them.

19. I appreciate me and my efforts to create a better life for myself.

Focus

20. I am focused on achieving my goal to (insert goal).

21. I pay attention to everything that goes on around me because I care.

22. My energy is focused on the task at hand; only then can I achieve my goals.

23. I am totally freed from any disruption.

24. I am in the state of flow and nothing can knock me off.

25. This task, concept, idea, etc. is very absorbing.

26. I am fully committed to achieving my goals because I am worth it.

27. I (name) embark on this activity with singular focus. So help me universe.

28. I have it good in life. I will focus on the positive and not the negative.

29. I am disciplined enough to finish doing this without

needless distractions.

30. I will not procrastinate. I will focus on doing this job until I am done, then I'll watch cat videos.
31. In the next two hours, nothing will occupy my mind but (insert very important task).

Excitement

32. I am excited to start living my ideal life!
33. If the universe is for me, who can be against me?
34. I will realize dreams and aspirations today.
35. I am sending positive energies into the universe right now.

Manifestations Exercises

Set Specific Intentions (Goals)

The most important part of expanding consciousness for the sake of manifesting is to understand exactly what you are aiming for. So, the very first exercise in accessing the superconscious should be to discover your life's purpose. Once you do this, you can create a great life vision and a number of goals to help you to achieve this one vision. Intentionality is very important when expanding consciousness. It harnesses your mental energy and directs it in one specific direction, usually the most suitable one for the realization of your dreams.

Make the Conscious Decision to Manifest Consciously

It is important that you tap into the superconscious and discover your purpose in life, because the next step in the conscious manifestation process is conscious decision. Here, you decide that you want to achieve something no matter what opposition you face. The only way you can follow through with this kind of decision is if you are 100% committed to the realization of a vision.

Harness the Desire

Desire is the driving force behind manifestation; the idea that if you want something badly enough, you can attract it into your life. Desire is the fuel that powers conscious manifestation. It is also what doubles as intention, or the aim to see something in your life that you have just seen in your mind.

Adjust Your Energy Fields Accordingly

Our thoughts produce vibrations of energy that in turn connect us to the universe for the purpose of manifesting. Dreams and desires can only be realized when they inspire positive thinking in the long run. If you dream and you desire yet your thoughts remain negative, you will only attract misery and misfortunes into your life. Negativity attracts negativity because it releases dark energy into the universe. Meditate, visualize, affirm, exercise gratitude; anything you can do to remain positive even when the situation pushes you in another direction.

Take Action

Save for a few isolated cases, manifestation does not negate the need for action. And like we mentioned earlier, the probabilistic nature of the world creates a situation whereby luck is created only by persistent and unrelenting work. This book gives you practical exercises to use in manifesting prosperity, but the actions you take will be the ultimate determinant of success. In fact, the best way to manifest is seeking to excel at the process rather than the outcome. This way, you will surely achieve excellence.

Speed Manifestation Techniques

The universe, in its infinite wisdom and infinite power, is infinitely just as mysterious. Even though you tap into to realize your dreams, you can never be sure when the manifestation exercises you are doing will bear fruit. You see, if you leave it open-ended, prosperity through the magic of the universe is something that could take years to appear in your life. In this section, we will look at the different techniques that you can employ to speed up the process of attracting.

First, you must believe that it is possible to speed up the delivery of your desired outcome. Ultimately, you are the one who decides what you want the universe to give you and when you want it. So, if you want a promotion in the next two months or a car within the next year, it is within your power to manifest these things. Now I know that I have advised against giving yourself a short time within which to get something, but this is only because the subconscious mind tends to have its own time frame. When you give yourself a shorter time, it revolts because it believes (based on previous experience) that it is impossible. But if you can tap into the superconscious – the part of the mind that is unlimited and all powerful, nothing is impossible!

The second thing to do is to keep your vibrations up. Tapping into the superconscious to manifest takes constant consciousness and an incessant invocation of the power of the universe. Use affirmations throughout the day, visualize, and be grateful. Practice meditation before bed and hypnotize yourself. Every moment of your day must be spent willing the thing you want into existence. To supersede the laws of the universe with a fast tracked request fulfillment, you have got to work for it. You must convince the universe that you want it badly enough – then go right ahead and take it.

The third step is to take inspired action. Even with speed manifestation when you tap into the heart of the universe – the superconscious – to receive your desires, action is still necessary. You will have to walk into your boss' office and request for a raise, buy a lottery ticket, or maybe apply for a grant, to get that money. In my previous speed manifestation exercises, I was amazed that so little initiative on my part produced such outstanding results. However, hardly have I ever seen something drop in my lap simply because I asked the universe for it. Take inspired action by planning everything out and then executing your idea as well as you can.

Finally, you must trust in the process. Sometimes your desires take awhile to manifest and oftentimes you will encounter obstacles. But if you are familiar with the Nova effect, you know that good luck sometimes comes disguised as bad luck. The worst mistake you could ever make when it comes to manifesting is to give up.

Chapter 2: Wealth

Now that we have established how manifestation works in general, let's get a little bit more specific. In this chapter, we will discuss the specific strategies through which you can manifest an abundance of money and other valuable assets into your life. We will focus on two specific manifestation strategies; affirmations and money mindset.

Affirmations for Wealth

The pursuit of money and valuable possessions has inspired many people to take action throughout history. In the last chapter, we discussed ways through which you can manifest money quickly to cover your financial needs. However, at the end of the day, money is only made in large enough quantities when you solve someone's problem and create value for them. Historically, the men and women who have accumulated vast amounts of wealth were those who created the most value for the world. From industrialists like Andrew Carnegie, to women like Estee Lauder, to innovators like Bill Gates, the world is full of perfect examples.

These men and women made it by dedicating their lives to providing value for their millions of customers. They were commanders of great business empires and the wealth they acquired was simply a reward for a job well done. If you want to start commanding the same level of self belief, joy in work, and wealth, affirmations are particularly effective there. They help you to harness the spirit of greatness that is inborn in all of us, realize your potential, and give you the drive to pursue your goal.

Affirmations for wealth start with the speaking which arouses your feeling. When you feel wealthy, your thoughts align and attract prosperity from the magic universe. So, the outcome of speaking wealth into your life is that you end up commanding it to manifest. It is a direct route. Below are 100 affirmations that will help you to awaken the greatness within, feel extra-motivated, achieve abundance, and manifest financial freedom in your life.

Awakening Greatness

Every one of us has been touched by the divine and been gifted with the unique ability to do things and achieve greatness. Many of us go through life without realizing that they have a piece of the universe, the divine being, or God in us. Instead of seeking to do great things and accumulating massive wealth, we seek simply to go through life without much difficulty. The graveyard is full of treasures because it has been filled with men and women who never achieved their greatest potential in life. They did not bring into the world the things that only they could.

When you aspire for more than just going through life in comfort, you must first discover and awaken the greatness within you. You must then aspire to reach the higher order of existence that the universe has placed within you. With purposeful affirmations, you eliminate all negativity from your mind and leave only the greatness within. This way, you get out of your own way, reach your dreams, and acquire massive wealth. Below is a list of powerful affirmations you can use to get yourself in the right position for exactly that.

1. I am the greatest man/woman of my kind to have walked the earth.
2. I am great!

3. I can do this!

4. I respect and love myself.

5. I am confident and self-assured.

6. I confidently express myself at all times.

7. No one can bring me down.

8. I am ready.

9. I will let nothing get in my way.

10. No one can stop me.

11. I am reaching for the sky.

12. The sky is no limit for me.

13. I am a genius.

14. I am incredibly gifted.

15. I have just the right blend of skills and competencies to achieve my loftiest goals.

16. I am a lion. Hear me roar!

17. I am a king/queen. Place a crown on my head!

18. I am the definition of awesomeness!

19. I am well on the way to realizing my greatest ambitions.

20. I can do anything I set my mind to.

21. I will reach my goals.

22. I will not fail.

23. Nothing can stop me.

24. I am a gift to mankind.

25. I have something special to give to the world.

26. I am the reason for my successes.

27. No one can do for the world what I am uniquely equipped to do.

28. I pursue knowledge relentlessly.

29. Everything I do is succeeding spectacularly.
30. I only do things the best way possible.
31. I give everything my best shot.
32. I have a magic touch.
33. I can do anything.
34. Everything I touch prospers.
35. I make my own luck.
36. I give everything my undivided attention.
37. I got this!
38. I'm ready for anything.
39. I am a winner!

Getting Motivation

Like I have said a few times now, action is vital to realizing your dreams even when you invoke the magic of the universe. To generate wealth, your actions must be inspired by a solid belief in the magic universe. The following affirmations will help keep you positive and motivated.

40. Every action I take is divinely inspired.
41. Everything I do takes me closer to my ultimate dream.
42. I am creative, determined, and motivated to achieve greatness.
43. I receive new opportunities to acquire wealth every day of my life.
44. It feels invigorating and stimulating to be out here pursuing my dreams!
45. I stay motivated even in turbulent situations.

46. I am exceeding my wildest expectations.

47. I am an inspiration to men and women out there.

48. I am confident in my abilities.

49. I will never quit!

50. I am surrounded by a supportive team of like-minded individuals.

51. I am determined to live a full life.

52. My purpose is my driving force.

53. Nothing can knock me off the path to my destiny.

54. I will keep moving forward.

55. I draw motivation from the deepest reaches of the universe.

56. I recharge my motivation easily.

57. Make it or make it. There is no but.

58. Giving up is not an option.

59. Hardships just make me want it more.

60. I work hard now so I can play later.

61. Yes I can!

62. I got this!

63. I fully trust that I can do this.

64. I believe in myself.

65. Every dream I am pursuing has already come true. I need only manifest it.

66. I am already the most successful version of me I can be. I just need to show it to the world.

67. I am playing my part in making the world a better place for everyone.

Abundance

This is the ultimate goal of tapping into the magic universe. In a limitless universe, the only cap to the things that you can achieve is usually yourself. To ensure that you achieve the highest possible levels of abundance, I have created a list of the most powerful affirmations. As you affirm these sentences over your life, remember that you don't lack because there is none, you lack because you don't pursue it. Awareness is the only difference between the haves and the have nots. As soon as you gain awareness and start asking for it, your whole life will turn around.

68. I am floating around in a universe filled with wealth.
69. I am growing richer every single day.
70. I am worthy of success and abundance.
71. It is incredible how easy it is to make money!
72. The rivers of wealth sure run deep in my life!
73. Money comes to me like metal to a magnet.
74. I am one with the Infinite Source of the universe.
75. I channel wealth from the Infinite Source.
76. I am the best custodian of wealth for the universe on earth.
77. I use my money well, make more, and spend it even better.
78. My mind is perfectly programmed to make money.
79. The doors are open for the wealth and prosperity I desire to flow into my life.
80. I have more money than I need.

81. It feels amazing to have this money.

82. I am financially secure (not insecure).

83. It feels good to be rich!

84. Oh, how grateful I am for all the wealth I possess!

85. I sparkle like a polished diamond!

86. I shine!

87. I am manifesting every item of my desire into my life right now.

88. I love making other people's lives better with my immense wealth

89. I am like a transformer. I receive wealth, step it up, and distribute it to the world.

90. My business prospers today more than it did yesterday.

91. I am the proprietor of the world's next unicorn.

92. I am the most successful employee in my company.

93. I am an important part of this company.

94. I am a positive light for others.

95. I am helpful.

96. I am leading this company to success.

97. The work I do touches lives and creates value for others.

98. I inspire my coworkers.

99. I work hard to achieve the results I expect.

100. My wealth is received on behalf of the world. I will use it to make it a better place.

Magnetic Money Mindset

The state of your mind plays an important part in manifesting wealth. See, it is very easy to let the negative energies and ominous predictions in the news and on social media trap you in a quagmire of negativity and defeatism. To attract money, you must be willing to go against the current of popular opinion as long as you flow with the magic of the universe. In fact, you can exploit the universal law of polarity to pivot negativity around you into positivity and maintain your strong hold on your vision.

A bad mindset can condemn you to a life in mediocrity and make it impossible for you to identify opportunities to make good money. As long as you are willing to think outside the box, maintain positivity, and endeavor to succeed in every situation, you can keep building wealth in recessions and booms. In this section, I will share with you the most effective tools for the discovery of your purpose. These tools will allow you to tap into your creative genius, do what you love, and attract financial freedom along the way.

Create a Vision

A vision is the first and most important requirement to develop a magnetic money mindset. It gives your life meaning and allows you to focus all your actions to the attainment of the most important thing. And using the magic of the universe, you can discover your life's purpose simply by accessing your superconscious. Thereafter, visualizations help to keep you focused on the task at hand. The task at hand is always in service to your vision and purpose in life.

Do Away with Small Annoyances

The smallest of annoyances are notoriously effective in draining your energy. They exist in our day-to-day life as minor inconveniences that may make you cuss, waste an extra minute or two of your day, but are often not serious enough to warrant immediate mitigation. For example, a slow Internet connection that slows you down as you try to catch up with work can spoil a good day at work or spoil your relaxation time if your entertainment videos buffer while you watch, and a cold shower because your heater is not working means a bad start to your day. Eliminating these small annoyances will rejuvenate you and increase your energy levels in a huge way. Moreover, living in a world where things work flawlessly inspires you to manifest the same in all other areas of your life, including your finances.

Respect Money

The people who make money are the ones who actually respect, value, and appreciate the things that it allows them to do in their own lives. Instead of looking at it like some inconvenience without which you can't live the life you want, start thinking of money as a means to an end, with the end being your perfect life and a better life for everyone who depends on you for their sustenance.

Respecting money encompasses the value you attach to it as well as the way you handle actual money when you earn it. Do you put the money in your wallet in a haphazard way or are the notes organized by value in a neat way? Is your wallet worn and ugly or is it a beautiful container for your valued cash? The latter indicates a serious view of and respect for money.

Save and Invest Your Money

There are three ways to handle your money after you make it. You can either spend it all, or you can set some of it aside for future use as saving. In savings, you can keep the money lying idly in the bank or you can make it work for you to make even more. You see, the bank does not keep all the money you save in a safe and await for you to withdraw it. They take it and invest in real estate, the stock markets, infrastructural projects, and other money-making avenues. Your savings enables them to do this, but what you receive is an insignificant share of their earnings.

But when you take your money and invest it yourself, you actually attract more to you like a magnet. Investments give you very high returns and because you don't have to be actively involved in making that money, it will serve as an additional stream of income adding even more to what you already have.

Don't Hoard Worthless Things

If you want to attract new things into your life, you can't hurry the process up by getting rid of old stuff. For example, you will never really focus on manifesting that car you have always wanted if you keep driving around in your old one. Somehow, the fact that you are still moving around in relative comfort means that a part of your mind will be pushing you towards settling for what you already have. But when you get rid of things you don't want, you create a vacuum where they used to be. Because nature abhors vacuums, it will send you the things you attract to fill up the vacuum!

Work on Your Strengths

The richest people in the world are those who understand their strengths and focus on exploiting them to the maximum. Instead of worrying about the things you don't have, focus instead on what you have. Become the best at it, and then delegate what you can't do to someone who can do it better. This is the mindset that has been used by the world's richest men and women to establish massive business dynasties.

Recharge

Everyone needs something to rejuvenate them. Whether it is a round of tennis a few times every weekend, a swim, or a drive, it is important to find something that energizes you and do it intentionally. This ensures that you release pent up energy and prevents the possibility of burning out, a common affliction of the "almost-there" that derails their success just before it happens.

Over-deliver

Nothing makes you feel better than performing better than your projections. When you schedule an activity for two weeks and do it in one and a half weeks or project to make a million and make two, the extra time or income is even more valuable because your mind did not expect it. It gives you a shot of motivation and a drug-like high that makes it addictive to go back there. Think about that; getting addicted to succeeding and overdoing yourself! It is the mindset that impresses managers and grows careers for the employed. In business, exceeding customer expectations is the surest way to beat the competition and become the best in the block.

Invest in You

Overachievers know that their most valuable asset is themselves. They go out of their way to make themselves better at what they do. They build skills and focus on growing because success is a state of being. Only when you keep investing in your own capabilities can you succeed in setting the standards, winning new customers, and moving up the corporate ladder.

Gratitude

Finally, developing a magnetic money mindset calls for gratitude for every good thing you got going for you. When you exercise gratitude, you attract even more wealth into your life. Complaining only generates negativity, so if you must, offer only constructive criticism. And in gratitude, you can invoke the magic of the universe over your life by giving to the less fortunate. Not only does this make you feel more fulfilled and happy, it also attracts the good energy of other people's gratitude to you.

Chapter 3: Love

It would be a hollow life indeed that you would live if you prospered in every other area of your life but had to endure it with no love. Yes, I said endure. There is no enjoyment in a life devoid of love. In this chapter, we will talk about manifesting love in your life.

Love Yourself

Here is something worthy of careful note; the magic of the universe is limited when it comes to other people. This is mostly because these people usually have their own desires and command their own desires. Your power ends where the next person's rights begin. This means that manifesting someone into your life who will show you love is next to impossible. You will have better luck working on becoming the person that attracts someone of your dreams.

Most of the materials that you will find – both online and in books – only discuss manifesting love from the world or for a relationship. But before you can even get to manifest the love of your life, you must first become the person that attracts him or her. The first thing to do to get there is to learn how to love yourself. Self-love makes you feel more confident and more positive. You take care of yourself first before others and appreciate yourself for who you are without comparing.

Only then will the universe begin to open up for you and start to work in your favor. Only with love in your heart can you display the kind of passion that compels the universe to give you what you want, however huge it is. But more importantly for this topic, attracting the love of your life begins with loving yourself. So this is where we will start the discussion.

Understand Yourself

So you are supposed to love yourself, but do you even understand who this 'self' is? It is very difficult to maintain positive attributes and to appreciate yourself when you don't have a good idea of who you are. Socrates famously said that "the unexamined life is not worth living." Even when meeting a new potential mate, the first thing we do is try to find out what the other person is all about. Basic questions establish common interests, compatibility in thinking patterns, and personality. So ask yourself, "What are you all about?" "What do you prize most in life?" "What is the purpose of your very existence?" Understand your strengths and weaknesses, your likes and pet peeves, purpose in life, and pretty much everything there is to know about you.

Start by examining your whole life. How have you gone through the different stages of life? How do you cope with challenges? Are you the same person you were ten, five, or three years ago? How have you grown and has the growth been positive or negative? Write a personal profile describing yourself. If you are not 100% proud of the person you are, work on it and seek to improve yourself every single day. This is the first step in becoming the person you need to be to manifest the love of your life.

Be Happy

Everyone deserves to find happiness. It is one of those things that make life lovely and keep you fulfilled and focused. Even as you seek to become a better person, find happiness in your current situation. Be grateful that you have reached the place where you are today instead of looking into the past or waiting around for the person you will be in the future, or when this or that happens. Find value within because it is there and be happy for what you have managed to do so far. If you can have fun alone and not feel like the whole world has abandoned you, this is a great indication. It boosts your self-confidence and makes you more assured that you can do what you need to do to reach the great new heights to which you aspire.

Even when you are single, enjoying your own company increases your value as a mate. Nobody wants to go out with a grouch, and nobody wants to date the person whose happiness depends on others. First find happiness alone, then your love will come to make that joy complete.

There is another reason why you should be comfortable, even happy, being alone. If you have been out and about in the dating world, then you are familiar with desperate people and the peril they face in attracting a suitable mate. If you are not comfortable being single, you will either say yes to the next person that comes along even if he or she is not good enough for you or let others take advantage of you. This will only make you miserable. It is much better to take a few months after a relationship to recuperate and reenergize before jumping into the next one.

Let Go of Judgment

In other words, forgive yourself. Everyone makes mistakes, but you are more than the mistakes you made in the past. One way to forgive yourself is to reflect, objectively, on the things that you feel you did wrong. You can seek to learn, but by no means should you judge. It is the past, after all, and you can do nothing to make it better. Only after this self-evaluation can you forget about the past and move on. When you stop judging yourself and learn from mistakes, your self-worth improves as well. With improved self-worth, you will become more confident and capable of loving yourself.

Another reason why you must forgive yourself for previous mistakes is that you will instead seek to punish yourself. People punish themselves by getting into abusive relationships, sabotaging themselves in good ones, and a host of other self-destructive behavior. As you prepare to meet your love, these are issues you should put to bed beforehand.

Understand Your Potential

Would you be so critical of yourself if you were someone else? Simply reminding yourself about the things that you have done in the future can increase your self-esteem, confidence, and self-love. If you keep an accomplishments journal, read through it and fall back in love with yourself. Appreciate the huge odds you have conquered to get where you are and, for once, focus on the positive instead of the negative. Because this is a common trap that people fall into; criticizing their mistakes and yet denying themselves the credit they so rightly deserve for good deeds.

When going through your previous accomplishments, celebrate yourself. Share with your friends, pop a bottle of champagne, and take a moment to be grateful. Where you deserve praise for a job well done, you should be the first person to congratulate yourself.

Give Yourself a Break

I mean this literally and figuratively. First off, don't be too hard on yourself. Even if you want to be better than everyone else, the reality is that the world will treat you like just another person. You will be met with resistance, challenges, and bad breaks. Don't expect yourself to crush them all. Some will be just as hard on you as they are for everyone else.

Secondly, literally take a break and relax all through the day, at least for a whole day every week, and for a week or more every year. A vacation, even at home or in a nearby town, can do you wonders. It is one way to reinforce the love that you have for yourself, but it also gives you time to reflect, take stock, and be grateful.

Trust Yourself

Trusting in your own capabilities and listening to your instincts is a good way to show self-love. Only you can know what is best for you, and the way you know this is by instinct. Your instinct has been protecting you since you were young and is fine-tuned to keep you safe in a turbulent world so always do what it tells you. Before you can trust others, you must learn to trust yourself.

Attract Love

So, now that you have learned how to love yourself, take it a step further. Let us talk about the exact strategies that will lead to you meeting, falling in love with, and getting the love of your ideal mate.

Visualize Your Ideal Partner

The best way to start this process is to start by asking yourself what you are looking for in the ideal partner. As in, what gap are you looking to fill? If you want someone to love you to fill the void left by lack of self-love, you skipped the process above and risk failure if you don't go back and take care of it. Understanding your own needs from a love interest makes it easier to manifest from the universe a person who meets your needs. Write down the various characteristics he or she must have for them to satisfy your needs. At this point, you are not minding too much about superficial things like looks, ethnicity, religion, etc. It is the need that person will fulfill in you that matters above all else. Follow this up with the kind of relationship you want, focusing on your own input and role. In short, what are you bringing to the table?

By focusing on what you want and not the fact that you want to get something, you train your mind on finding the most suitable route to get you there. When you focus on the latter, you will instill in your mind the fact that you lack and exacerbate the situation.

Send out the Mating Call

Now that you know what you want and what you are offering, you can send the intention to the universe. The mating call means that you take action to meet your ideal lover. If it is those online dating sites, create a profile, if you have a crush or just someone you kind of like, approach him or her. Another very effective way to find love is to search for it within your social groups. Your friends might know someone who might be good for you, but if you keep preaching your singlehood or acting like someone who is not interested, they will probably never take the initiative. Shrug off your fear of being judged, announce it to your friends, and explore away!

Too much timidity might lead to you missing out on a good relationship simply because you were not courageous enough to put yourself out there. Women are especially prone to passivity while attracting a mate, probably because we live in a society that frowns on any perceived 'easiness' on the part of the woman. You can still send clear signals of your availability while still maintaining your dignity. Non-verbal cues are more effective in communicating interest in relationships than words.

Be Open

Sometimes you get out there only to find that your heart has a whole new idea of the kind of person you should be spending your life with. The process of finding love cannot be accomplished through mind alone. So even with your list, you must be ready to accept what the universe sends you. The secret is to listen to your heart, because the heart knows what it wants. Moreover, the actual process of meeting, getting acquainted with, and developing feelings for another person, is an important part. You will have to adapt, change some aspects of your personality, and probably even compromise on some aspects to get love.

When you let someone into your life, they revive something in you that was hidden and show you new parts of your personality that only they have the key to unlocking. Just because you like to spend your weekends watching a movie or partying does not mean that you have to find someone with the exact same interests. You might find that you would be just as happy hiking or mountain-climbing. Keep an open mind and be willing to experience life through the other person. Now this does not mean that you completely give up everything you love just to accommodate him or her, but you must be willing to compromise on some things.

It Does Not Work on Specific People

When you try using the magic of the universe to make someone fall in love, it means that not only are you imposing yourself on a person you are probably not compatible with, you are also imposing your will on the universe. This could be dangerous for a couple of reasons. First, the universe is the divine wisdom and it knows what you need. When you impose, you trust your own flawed conscious thinking beyond your own subconscious and superconscious, which are the real stores of knowledge.

Focusing only on one person makes you blind to other people who might be better suited to you. You reject the potential perfect love for the one person you are hung up on, which is just desperation. The more you try to attract a specific person in your life, the more likely you are to whittle yourself down to do so. You neglect your own needs and, as soon as the honeymoon period is over, you will probably end up jaded and unsatisfied. However, when you let the universe take care of you, you will never be sorry.

The Inner Love Flow

The inner love flow is a reminder of your deepest, most innate connection to the infinite source that provides you unconditional love. It is a concept through which hearts can be healed and faith restored. Simply by tuning into the present moment, listening to the heartbeat, and paying attention to the flow of air inside the body, you feel more alive, more grounded in the present moment, and more connected to the universe.

Sensing the inner flow allows you to re-establish connections with people you love through understanding, tolerance, and compromise. So, instead of thinking and doing things that benefit you alone, you start applying your efforts more and more to the things that benefit everyone around you. The inner love flow will be a constant reminder that it all starts with you and that you are never alone. If you want to tune into the power of the universe, first understand that it is an interconnected array of energy emitted from everything and everyone in the universe. The more positive connections you tap into, the greater the power you command.

Unconditional Love

Tapping into the inner love flow awakens unconditional love in our lives. When the aspects of the natural elements: Earth, fire, water, and air are balanced inside you, your heart attracts the power of the universe. The connection formed between you and the universe generates a flow of unconditional love going both ways. The connection that you feel with the universe in moments of mindfulness meditation, watching a beautiful sunrise, or listening to the flow of water down the river is part of unconditional love. It also comes from moments of bliss with other people. It allows you to form a strong bond and create a healthier relationship.

It would be quite impossible to give or experience unconditional love without balancing the elements within you. However, by balancing the Chakras and practicing Ayurvedic inner healing, you will open your heart to the universe and attract boundless love.

Using Consciousness

The superconsciousness is another thing that you can tap into to manifest love in your life. As the part of you that is rooted in the infinite source, the superconscious gives you a way to improve your love life by improving yourself. Not only will this make you the ideal partner for the love of your life, it also improves the quality of your life in profound ways. In this section, we will discuss a few ways in which superconsciousness meditation can help you achieve abundance in your love life.

Heal Your Heart from Any past Pains

At the deepest part of your heart, no pain exists. You are freed from all past suffering, hold no grudges, and experience the world from a position of purity of heart. The subconscious and conscious parts, however, are choking with past wrongdoings and grudges. These grudges affect the quality of not just your life, but your love life as well. It is not uncommon for relationships to suffer because one person still has baggage from previous relationships that bar them from forming a deeper relationship with their partner. We carry into adulthood pains from our childhood. These long past memories of neglect, lack, and/or rejection affect the way we act in different situations. And because these issues are rooted in the subconscious, it is rather difficult to uproot them. The superconscious is the only viable route.

Form a Deeper Connection with Your Partner

A heart that is in touch with the superconscious is a heart that is capable of receiving and channeling unconditional love. This is the same love that is invoked in marriage, so if you want to form such a connection, it might help to tap into the superconscious. It allows you to love yourself for the person you are and accept your partner with all the flaws he or she has. True forgiveness also comes from the subconscious and giving it to yourself and your partner elevates your relationship higher.

Chapter 4: Friendships

Lonely is the person who walks through life with no companions. Indeed, friends fulfill a very basic need for companionship. And even though love fades, friendships – at least the true and best kind – last forever. You can survive through life in considerable peace without romantic love, but it would be a sad life indeed that you would live were you to go through it with no friends. In this chapter, we will look at the different types of friendships that exist, the metrics for measuring true friendships, benefits of true friendship, and practical ways to make friends. Our focus on understanding what friendship is all about is intentional because a true friend is one type of relationship that comes most naturally. Too much focus on how to become (or attract) a good friend and we will have little chance of forming true friendships.

Types of Friendships

Our discussion on the types of friendships will be based on the ideas of Greek Philosopher Aristotle. In the essay *Nicomachean Ethics*, he devoted some space to defining friendships as being based on utility, pleasure, and the good.

Friendships by utility are based on mutual benefit. It is a *quid pro quo* sort of relationship- in other words. The whole premise of the friendship is that you both benefit. So, even if you don't go around keeping score, you know that you can always count on the person's help should you need it in the future. Spoken or unspoken, utility exists in every friendship. After all, you don't want a friend who will abandon you in your hour of need.

Friendship of pleasure is another kind of platonic relationship that is mainly based on the enjoyment of each other's company. The people with whom you go out partying, watching a football game, or hit the beach with are your pleasure buddies.

Finally, we have friendships by kin. These are the kinds of friendships in which your relationship is based on mutual respect and interest in each other's life. Family members and blood relations are prime candidates for this kind of friendship, even though it doesn't always happen. Sometimes, the bond just isn't strong enough and you only to relate to each other as much as you have to.

Kin friendships are also the kind of relationship that BFFs (meaning best friends forever) enjoy. It is a more powerful and lasting relationship based on common goals, values, and visions for life. You can rely on the other person for direction and support in the most important area of your life – your purpose. These kinds of friendships usually start in childhood or adolescence when two or more people come together almost by chance, only to form a bond as strong as kinship. It is much easier to have unconditional love with kin friends.

Of course, few friendships can stand on just one of the pillars discussed above. The kind of friendship that BFFs have encompasses all three types of friendships discussed above. You will definitely enjoy each other's company, pursue the same interests, and have a good time. Just as important is the spoken or unspoken promise to always have each other's back. When you are in trouble, the first person you are most likely to seek out is the kin type because their help is unconditional. The friendships of pleasure and utility are more or less convenient by nature. You form them when you need them, but as soon as it is no longer convenient, they fade away into the past.

Tenets of Good Friendships

Naturally, it is the last kind of friendship that you should strive to attract into your life. And just like romantic love, manifesting friendships starts with becoming the perfect version of the person you want to attract into your life. The universe is naturally aligned to bring like and like together, so when you attract friends, it is the sum total of your energy (personality) that will attract.

So in this section we will discuss the qualities of friendships that allow you to gain mental and spiritual rejuvenation. These are the qualities that make friends who push you forward in the quest to achieve your goals and meaning in life.

Empathy

Relating to someone's tribulations may not completely eliminate their pain, but it makes it less lonely and thus lessens the pain. Empathy requires the ability to put yourself in someone else's shoes and walk a mile in them. If you can get a better understanding of what it is like to be someone else, you will be a much better friend.

The first and most important skill required in empathy is active listening. When someone is talking about something important, ask questions, nod along, express interest. It builds trust and strengthens the connection between the two of you.

Selflessness

The ability to care deeply about a friend's plight is necessary for true, kin friendships. Thinking only about yourself can be tempting, but it does not form a very good foundation for relationships. Showing concern for someone else's problems and struggles in life is what shows someone that you care. This includes doing whatever you can to make their life easier by solving their problems and helping out where you can. As an element of utility friendships, that last quality of true friendship strengthens even further the bond of true friendship.

Trustworthiness

Trust is very important for true friendship. It encompasses being able to keep someone's deepest secrets and confidential information to material things. So, the question to answer would be: Can you be trusted to keep a secret for a friend? How big a secret would that be? The bigger the secret you can keep, the greater the confidence you will inspire from your strongest friends.

Material trustworthiness also counts for a lot. So, can you be trusted to guard a highly treasured object if you would never be found if you broke that trust? If you can remain faithful in spite of material gain for doing otherwise, your value as a friend will be all the greater.

Interests

When two friends have common interests, they will never tire of each other's company. Whether it is an interest in the arts, business, politics, or religion, shared interests is the glue that holds friendships together for life. Spending time with someone who enjoys the same stuff that you do can be beneficial because you never have to compromise with the activities. As good as compromise might otherwise be, we all know that it is much more fulfilling to do what you really want to do. Friends with whom our interests and life goals are aligned make prime candidates for a mastermind relationship, which can be infinitely fulfilling.

A Different Perspective

When you spend all your time with someone who doesn't challenge you, you will become staid in your ways even if they are wrong. So, as much as common interests are great, some distinction can be even better. A good friend will always offer a new perspective to issues and open your eyes to new ways of thinking or doing things. Find a friend who helps you grow and become a better person each day and you will have found an indispensable kin.

This aspect of true friendship is called destiny shaping. It entails a concerted effort to help someone achieve their goals. You want to become the friend who will move earth and seas to make a friend's dreams come true. You also want to find that friend.

Respect

Everyone feels good when they are respected by people they hold with high esteem. The mutual respect aspect of true friendship therefore plays a huge part in the overall health of the relationship. Respect from a friend increases the self-confidence you have as well as your self worth. So, even when tackling seemingly huge problems, you will do so much better when a friend is at the sidelines cheering you on.

Loyalty

Loyalty is probably the most important aspect of true friendship. It ties everything together neatly. In essence, the level of loyalty a friend shows is determined by their performance on all the aspects discussed here. So, a loyal friend will support you at all times regardless of their opinions on what you are doing. And if they disagree with your actions, they will advise you to do the right thing. They keep your confidence, go out of their way to accommodate your needs, and be by your side during the hardest moments of your life.

Benefits of Mastermind Friendships

True friendship has numerous benefits. Not only does it improve mental well-being, it also allows us to maintain a good emotional state. However, when it comes to friendships and the universe, we must focus on the form of friendship discussed by Napoleon Hill in *Think and Grow Rich*: mastermind friendships. A mastermind relationship is a friendship where common interests align and two or more people commit to become each other's destiny shapers. This is why it is also called a destiny friendship because the aim is to help each other achieve goals and visions.

A single mind vibrates with enough strength to attract marvelous things from the universe. When common interests align in a mastermind relationship, the vibrations increase exponentially. This makes it much easier to manifest the things everyone in the relationship desires. The benefits to be accrued from joining a destiny shaping friendship include:

Accountability

A mastermind friendship entails the sharing of goals and visions. Once a goal has been shared with another person, it becomes a lot more concrete. First off, you receive the feedback and advice of someone you trust pertaining to your pursuits. Second, the person becomes your accountability partner, keeping up with your progress on the goal, and pushing you to work harder.

Increased Focus and Clarity

In a mastermind relationship, all members have their own goals to pursue. Some measure of competition ensues, because you don't want to be the only person to never reach your goal. You will focus more and work harder to make sure that you keep the pace of everyone else. Clarity comes from the availability of fresh perspectives to every challenge you face.

Confidence

A mastermind relationship entails consultation with a trusted friend. You will be assured of receiving insightful advice and well-meaning guidance on every problem. Therefore, you will see a substantial increase in your decision-making capabilities and with it, greater confidence in your own abilities. You can expect, therefore, to be even more inspired than ever to continue pursuing your dreams.

Superior Thinking

When you are in a mastermind or destiny friendship, you always have someone with whom to discuss new ideas and brainstorm solutions to problems. This leaves you with less room for defeatist thinking and opens your mind to new possibilities. Your mindset becomes money magnetic and driven towards growth. The bigger you are willing to aim, the greater the chances you have of actually succeeding.

Greater Vibration Energy

This is the principal benefit of destiny relationships. They prop up your own mind and make it easier for you to attract the magic of the universe in your life. As long as you remain strong and don't allow negative energies to interfere with your own manifestation, you can achieve so much greater things when there is another like-minded person attracting the same thing as you. This is the innate power of the mastermind group as discussed by Napoleon Hill.

How to Make Good Friendships

Now, we have talked about the types, qualitative, and benefits of destiny friendships. The latter is a unique sort of friendship that allows us to align our dreams with our friends and improve our link with the universe. Thereafter, we will have greater power to manifest. In this section, we will get into the finer details of manifesting friendships. These are tips that work for utility, pleasure, and destiny friendships because it doesn't matter so much how you run your friendship as the fact that you actually do get friends. That is to say that you can attract someone into your life, but you can't really dictate the sort of relationship you will have with them. These interpersonal aspects tend to take their due course, by and large.

The short answer to the question, "how do I manifest friends in my life?" is that you must live by the tenets of good friendships discussed earlier. When you are a good friend, you will induce your friends to treat your right by the principle of reciprocity. However, we all know that it is a little bit more complicated than that. So, in this section, let's focus on the process of making a good friend.

Know Thyself

Just like the unexamined life is not worth living, so is a friend who does not know who they are not worth having. Nothing is more disastrous that finding out years later that your friend simply adopted your dreams and goals and neglected finding his or her true purpose. Well, unless it is being on the other side of that scenario. This happens and it wrecks friendships. Understand yourself, find out what you life mission is, come up with a crude idea of how to get there, THEN attract the friends to help you get there.

Understand What You Want

If you are an introvert who wants to experience more of the extrovert world or an extrovert who wants to taper your extraversion qualities, a person who meets these qualities is a great place to start. Friends are very useful for attaining balance in our lives. Just as useful as experiencing new spheres of the world that have remained closed to you. Determine the need you want a friend to fulfill in your life so that you can focus your mind on attracting exactly the right person for you.

Be the Person You Want to Be Friends With

This has been said more than once in this chapter alone, but it is so important it deserves a section all of its own. If you want to know the kind of person you are, look at your friends. If you want to know why you have the friends you have, look in the mirror. Your friends are a reflection of you, so if you want to get better friends, look within first.

Give More Than You Receive

This is a great tip to help you keep your friendships strong. Always aspire to be a better friend to the best of best friends and you will see your relationship blossoming more and more each day.

Release Toxic Friends

Toxic friends can derail you in your quest to achieve your goals. With their negative views of life and lack of ambition, they will slowly but surely drain your power to manifest, break your connection with the universe, and scatter your dreams to the winds. You deserve to have friends who support you rather than pull you down and you must be strong enough to let the latter go.

Join Groups

Sometimes you need to actually go out of your way to make new friends. If you keep yourself locked up and never socialize, your chances of meeting a great new friend are very minimal. Especially with mastermind friendships, the process of making friends is quite formal and deliberate. You can join groups on social media, make friends, and take it offline if need be. This is not one of those situations when you can afford to be shy. The benefits of meeting a destiny shaper far outweigh the momentary discomfort you will feel while getting acquainted with your new friend.

Chapter 5: Success

Abundance in life also means positive outcomes in everything that you do. This is the wholesome definition of success, one that goes beyond the profusion of money and possessions. Sure, money is a key metric for success, but it is not the only one. In this chapter, we will discuss the different strategies you can use to ensure that everything you do succeeds by tapping into the magic of the universe.

Clear Mental Blocks

Your own mind could be the very thing standing between you and success in attracting the magic of the universe and manifesting your desires in life. Some of these mental blocks include:

Stop Overthinking Small Things

Every big project, every major goal, every vision, are all achieved through the consistent and constant fulfillment of small tasks. When you spend too much time thinking about these small tasks, you will end up spending an uneconomical amount of time working towards your goals. The outcome of this affliction, especially in the creative industry, is procrastination. And the more you procrastinate, the more you attract negative thoughts and sabotage your own chances at success. Think of these small tasks like steps in a journey to a destiny (the goal). Once you have figured out the road to reach the destination, you don't think about every step you take. Once you make a decision to do something, the execution should follow with no delay.

When you overcome this mental block to the smaller tasks, you will be more focused on attracting the goal. And because it is much easier to succeed in these smaller tasks, you will have more accomplishments to celebrate about. These celebrations generate positive vibrations and boost your power to generate favorable results in everything that you do.

Douse the Fires of Doubt

Another mental block that hinders your success in life is doubts. Doubts are caused by rational and irrational fears, but they result in low confidence and poor self-esteem. The negativity that results in these emotions blocks the power of our minds and makes it harder to manifest abundance in any area of our lives.

The trick when dealing with self-doubt is to douse them with affirmations or mantras before they take root. The best time to deal with doubt is at the very onset. On top of the affirmations, you must also take action. Keeping yourself busy with productive work is the most effective way to overcome fear. Once you overcome the fear within, you will have succeeded in uprooting the doubts at their source.

Don't Fear Failure

You cannot separate failure and success. In fact, I dare you to find someone who has never encountered failure in their life. Every successful man or woman in the world has his or her own story of how they had to overcome failure to get where they are today. So, do not fear failure, because only by going through failure can you become the person who actually succeeds. As long as you remember that you are not a failure until you stop trying, you can undertake any project and achieve anything you set your mind to achieve.

Simplify

Have you ever been in a situation where you were struggling to do something but could not get around to doing it because something in your mind was holding you back, only to have the obstacle removed by simplifying the situation? Sometimes the brain gets trapped in complexity and fails to function properly, leading to procrastination, freezing, the fear of failure (and success) among other challenges. The simplest way to do something is usually the quickest, cheapest, and most effective.

Ensure that you have a clear view of the goal and eliminate distractions and you will be on your way to discovering the secret for an unobstructed mind. Only by simplifying can you truly unlock the mind's power and attract the magic of the universe to find success in everything that you do.

Don't Get Cocky

Overconfidence is one thing that thwarts many people in the quest for success. It happens when too much favorable outcomes makes you feel invincible. With notions of invincibility comes a self-destructive sort of carelessness that always results in mistakes and failures. Keep your eye on the prize and adjust your goals when it appears that your previous aim was too low. This way, your focus remains razor-sharp and you keep attracting the magic of the universe to succeed in every area of your life.

Eliminate Limiting Beliefs

You could be the reason why you are not succeeding in life. Let us take a moment to let that sink in. You work so hard, dedicate so much time and money into your goal, but the reason why you don't get what you were working for ends up being YOU. When you think, even at the subconscious level, that you can't achieve something, your mind attracts failure and disappointment from the universe. It is a self-fulfilling prophecy that has been sinking dreams and aspirations as long as man has been having dreams and aspirations.

Low Self-worth

This limiting belief man leads to men and women of tremendous potential who walk around thinking that they are not good enough to reach their goals. When your self-worth is low, you will tend to walk around feeling worthless and being miserable. Even when you do achieve something, the voice at the back of your mind will make you feel like an imposter and you won't really enjoy your victory. You need to start believing that you are worthy to receive the biggest blessings from the universe, because you do. But at the end of the day, your beliefs must change, because if they don't, you will find yourself trapped in failure, unable to do anything to save yourself.

Whether you think you can or you think you cannot, you are absolutely right. I rest my case.

Not for the Likes of Me

People who go around thinking like this might be very secure in the notion that they at least believe in themselves. You know, to a certain extent. They know they can do something, just not THE thing that everyone will be talking about. It is just as bad as complete lack of belief in your abilities and must be overcome with positive reinforcements and superconscious meditation. The only thing to which you should be saying "not for the likes of me" is moderate success. You are the kind of person who achieves beyond and above anyone's expectations.

My Health Cannot Let Me

Unless you are lying in bed strapped to an oxygen tank and IV drip, this is just an excuse that you are using to avoid having to give your current goal everything you got. It is imperative that you take care of your body through exercise, proper dieting, and take care of your body to preserve it in good health for as long as you can. Not only does this keep you feeling fit and healthy, it also keeps you energetic as you pursue your dreams. Nothing, not even sickness, can stop you from doing something unless you let it. When you search within, you will always find some reserve of energy and motivation through which you can power your spirit and achieve your goals, regardless of what stands in your way.

I Am Not Rich Enough

The number of people who were born into poverty and rose to command multi-billion dollar fortunes is big enough that this self-limiting belief should be comparatively easy to overcome. And while it is a very powerful self-limiting belief, keep in mind that money is not the only thing that is needed for success. Neither is it the metric through which success is measured. With determination and hard work, you will realize your dreams sooner or later. The universe will see to it.

Visualize What You Want

Visualization is one of the most effective ways to achieve success in everything that you do. When you visualize, you use your mind to communicate to the universe the desires of your heart. By practicing mindfulness visualization and filling every waking moment of your day with the pictures of your future success, you leave the universe with no choice but to give you what you want. However, visualization does not just attract the magic of the universe to you, when you visualize, you also get yourself in the right state of mind to receive from the universe. In this section, we will discuss the actions you need to take to ensure that you come out of the process with exactly what you desire.

Set Clear Intentions

Here, you must define exactly what you want from the manifestation process. This you can do by tapping into the superconscious and envisioning the perfect world for you. What does it look like? Whatever images you get should be the vision you pursue for the rest of your life. It is your purpose in life and must be pursued with every ounce of your energy.

When you have decided what you want your future to look like, focus on that image and internalize it. Make sure that you see that goal everywhere you look. That is to say, live in a state of constant and never-ending awareness of your vision. You should be able to visualize that perfect future with little effort whether you are using the magic of the universe to attract love, wealth, friendships, health, peace, or happiness. In fact, create a vision where you have all these things in your life. That is what true success is all about. And if you visualize it and believe that you deserve it, the universe will have no option but to grant it to you.

Interact with Success

If you spend too much time in a destitute environment, your idea of what constitutes as success gets worryingly low. This is because the mind adjusts to this environment and in a somewhat misguided bid to save you from pining, lowers your ambitions. So, go out into the world. Read about the world's best achievers. Interact with the most ambitious person you can find out there. Take a moment to envision the possibilities of abundance that your life could have. Unless the vision to which you are working makes you anxious, go back to the drawing board. Come up with such an audacious vision that you are a little (or a lot) scared that it is impossible. That is the vision that you should work towards.

Live It out in Advance

The secret to visualizations that result in success is to experience your success even before it comes to you. When you visualize, it does help a lot to make it as realistic as possible by seeking to experience the full-dimensional experience. Notice the colors, feel the textures, smell the fragrances, get the full emotional experience every time you close your eyes to imagine the future. When you do this, the visualization becomes innate to your subconscious mind. It is much easier to tap into the superconscious and manifest your dreams when your subconscious is already in play.

Actually Attract Your Success

Sometimes the reason why our dreams have not come true is simply because we spend too much time chasing away the scarcity instead of pulling our dreams home. Pulling is easier than pushing- everyone knows that. So when you try pushing your troubles out instead of pulling success into your life, the universe does not necessarily notice the difference. You end up attracting misery. Other psychological reasons why you are attracting the wrong things into your life include:

Confirmation Bias

Even though you are confident that you will succeed, there is still a little part of your mind that remains doubtful. If you are not careful, confirmation bias could make you wreck your whole vision by taking in the parts of events in your life that confirm your negative beliefs. Confirmation bias is the basis for which "omens" are founded. You assign the meaning that your mind wants you to assign to something based on your own beliefs.

If you are to have any confirmation bias in your pursuit for success, make them positive, confirming the manifestation of the things you want in your life. It does not really indicate anything, but it is harmless enough. Sooner or later, you will see your dreams come to pass.

The Texas Sharpshooter Fallacy

This is another thought pattern whereby we shift our thinking to assign meanings that suit us to random events. It is based on the story of a man who randomly shoots at a barn first and then paints a target to show that he has a good shot. Avoid assigning meaning to 'signs' from the universe that have nothing to do with your manifestation exercises. Continuing along this part makes you anxious and impatient. Soon enough, negative thoughts and doubts creep up and you start to manifest failure and mediocrity.

Self-fulfilling Prophecies

This is a very common risk that many people treat casually or don't pay enough attention to. We make numerous prophecies about the future. Sometimes they are about small things like a night out or a date, but sometimes they are generated by a scary prospect. "Ooh, Nick outperformed me this quarter; he is going to get promoted, not me." "Oh no, I messed up the terms of that contract agreement. I am going to lose so much money on this!"

The interesting thing about self-fulfilling prophecies is that they make us spectators in our own lives. The scary thing about them is that they make us cheer for the other team. Instead of interpreting setbacks as your damnation, focus instead on what you can do to make everything work out fine. You will be surprised to find that it is not even as dire as you had led yourself to believe.

Meditate

In a world that is full of stress and turbulence, meditation is one thing you can do to improve your peace of mind and balance. However, balance and peace of mind is not the only thing that meditation brings. Studies have shown that meditation helps prepare you for success in every area of life and it is practiced by prominent personalities like Oprah Winfrey, Ray Dalio, and actor Will Smith among others (Mindworks Team, 2019). As it pertains to promoting a successful life, the benefits of meditation include:

It Enhances Memory and Learning

When you meditate, you alter the structure of your brain and boost its agility. The memory processing parts in particular gets a shot of vigor every time you meditate. This means that your ability to process and recall new material will improve, as will your efficiency.

Helps Overcome Pessimism

During meditation, we unlock and access the subconscious or superconscious areas of our minds. So, if you are to repeat a positive mantra over and over again during your meditation, you will dissipate the negative thought loops in your mind and make it possible for your mind to focus on other, more important, things.

It Builds Your Mental Capacity

When you meditate, you give your brain a workout that makes it stronger, more accurate, and focused. This will allow you to retain the sharpness and capacity of your brain even when others' brains are deteriorating later on in life. And in the present time, meditation helps you to be more attentive to details and to think accurately.

Eliminating Negative Emotions

When you meditate, you process and accept negative emotions rather than denying their existence or influence on your life. This is especially true for mindfulness meditation, which examines every thought and dismisses it and moves on to the next one. So, when you meditate, you will finally be empowered to rein in those outbursts of emotion that have been straining your relationships with a partner, colleagues, or friends.

Emotional Resilience

When you meditate, you take the time to scrutinize your emotions. This allows you to examine the way your actions affect the people around you. Your resilience grows, as does your ability to recover from bad moods. This has the net effect of making you a better communicator and strengthening your relationships with the people close to you. So, instead of responding to other people's words and actions in a knee-jerk manner, we take a moment to feel the resultant emotions and respond in a calm and measured way.

Less Anxiety

Human beings are programmed to react to stress through fight or flight. When we are stressed, the heightened blood pressure, accelerated heartbeat, and faster breathing tend to create long-lasting harm to your health. When you meditate, you improve your response to stress and avoid these potentially harmful reactions. It also improves your tranquility and quality of sleep that you get at the end of the end, which is also important for mental, emotional, and physical health.

More Creativity

To succeed, you will need to be creative about the way you handle challenges and nurture ideas. This way, you will be better placed to deal with hurdles to your success. Mindfulness meditation makes it possible for us to entertain thoughts without judging or trying to control them. It also allows you to accept what you are feeling and become more cognitively flexible.

Chapter 6: Health

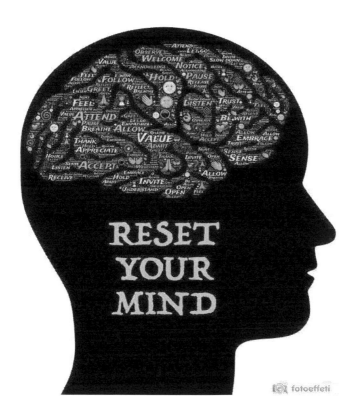

Without good health, it would be impossible to enjoy all the things we have discussed here. In fact, poor health might even make it harder to manifest. Not only does it generate pain and emotional stress, it also saps our energy and makes it much harder to focus on anything else. You need complete wellness to be in a true state of abundance in life.

Now most people think of wellness only in its physical aspects, but that is just one of its dimensions. Perfect health requires perfect wellness in the intellectual, emotional, spiritual, and social areas of life. Only when you have attained wellness in these five areas can you be in perfect health. All these aspects of health are interlinked, which means that poor health in one of the areas results in poor health in other areas as well. In this chapter, we will look at the different strategies that you can use to manifest perfect health from the universe.

Physical Health

Physical health is basically the vitality of all our organs. When any part of the body is in poor shape or entirely dysfunctional, the whole body suffers.

Know What You Want

Whether you want to have a healthier body aesthetically or heal an illness, you can tap into the magic and manifest your desire over your life. But to make this possible, you must define exactly what you want. This is the first secret of using the power of the mind to attract health from the magic universe.

The idea here is that you must think about the things that being in good health will bring you. This way, it is not just physical fitness that you are looking for, you are looking for the vitality and power that comes with it. And when you seek to be free from disease, your mind is healthy and your body is primed to pursue your ideal life.

Visualize

Visualizations help you to attract good health because they help you to start seeing yourself as healthy even before you actually get there. This helps you to increase the frequency of your vibrations and align your energies to the universe. With repetition, visualization works as a simulator and has been found to produce the same impact as physical practice in basketball players. It commands all other parts of the body to fall in line so that what you visualized may come to be. However, you must remember that practical actions are needed as well, and visualization alone does not work when it comes to physical health. You must augment it by hitting the gym, the racing track, or seeing the doctor.

Believe

You must believe that it is possible to stay healthy and fit for it to happen. This means that you must eliminate all the little doubts and second thoughts. Failure to do this will result in half-hearted attempts that will probably fail. Only when you enhance your belief can you succeed in removing the blocks that stand between you and living a healthier life.

And in showing your beliefs, actions speak louder than words. If you can't bring yourself to put in the work needed to attain perfect physical health, then perhaps some part of your subconscious is in doubt. Until you clear up these doubts, you might end up procrastinating on a healthier life long into the future.

Gratitude

Being grateful really gives you a fresh perspective to life. When you are dissatisfied with the kind of body you have, it is something that stays with you, poisoning every moment of the day. You go out to the store, glance at your reflection, and you are reminded of it all over again. The glances people give you make you feel judged even if they are not judgmental. All this negativity makes it very hard for you to practice gratitude, but it is what you need to do to turn it all around. If you can find one thing to be thankful for in the way you look, you can build up on it and actually get the body you want.

Work for It to Receive It

Whether you are looking for better physical fitness or good health, wishing for it and visualizing will hardly ever be enough. You must exercise to lose weight, get toned muscles, and improve your body's vitality. Without these actions, you will remain in your current rut for a long time yet.

As for health, seeing a doctor is just one way to receive healing. Modern medicine can take care of most of the common diseases that we suffer. However, you can also tap into the magic of the universe to cure yourself of diseases by practicing visualized meditation. In *The Secret*, Rhonda Byrne tells the story of John Assaraf who cured his body of ulcerative colitis. John used the mind to visualize his body healing itself from a cellular level. This process works even faster and more effectively than conventional medicine. It is also cheaper and risk-free because the mind understands exactly what is wrong with the diseased part. The healing process happens automatically as soon as the superconscious experiences the vibrations of your thoughts.

Spiritual Health

Spiritual health is the measure of your connection with God or a higher power, the self, and nature. Spiritual wellness plays a part in the state of your physical health as well. When you are well connected with the inner self, you are in a better place to respond to signs of ill health.

The key to creating a connection with a higher power is prayer or meditation depending on your idea of a higher being. If you are a believer of God, prayer keeps you connected and in communication, which enables you to get your needs fulfilled. In essence, prayer works the same way that meditation works to connect you with the universe. And in reaching God through prayer, you reach for the same universal mind that meditation connects us to.

Spiritual health is even more important in the current world where chaos, social strife, and environmental destruction are increasingly creating a disconnect between the self and others, a higher being, and Mother Nature. Urban living, for one, creates a vast disconnect with nature. What with the glare of streetlights at night, honking of cars, and aerial living, we rarely ever look up to behold the night sky.

This disconnect between man and nature means that environmental issues mean less to us at the very time when we should be more concerned. Studies show that ten thousand species go extinct and more than ten million hectares are cleared every year. At that rate, the world is headed for some serious trouble in the future. When you are spiritually balanced, you start to understand more and more that we are all part of one whole with the environment. Letting this destruction continue to go unchecked is an act of self-destruction because it will ultimately end up hurting us all.

Specifically, the following are some excellent ways to improve spiritual health by tapping into the magic of the universe. Remember, when it comes to spirituality, the universe is everything that surrounds us, both seen and unseen.

- Discover the spiritual core. The essence of all humans is spirit. This innermost part of us gives our lives meaning. So when you explore it, you understand the essence of your existence.
- Find deeper meaning to everything in life. Everything has a deeper meaning; we just fail to pay attention. Spiritual well-being entails probing patterns of behaviors, especially those that hold us back. At the end of it all, you will realize that your destiny is closer than you ever thought and you play a bigger part in its fulfillment than you imagined.
- Take a few minutes to meditate every day. When seeking to manifest abundance from the universe, meditation is crucial. It helps us to reconnect with our superconscious mind and recharge after a long day of negativity and stress.
- Get out into nature. As I mentioned above, urban living can be very choking to the spiritual well-being because it cuts our connection to Mother Nature. It is a good idea to

take the time out to reconnect by spending a day or two out in the wild.

Without spiritual well-being, all other aspects of your health are likely to deteriorate as well. Spiritual health is what ties them all together. Even the transcendental healing used to heal the body that we touched on above requires a robust spirit. You cannot get healing for an ailing body from a spirit that is itself contaminated.

Emotional Well-being

Emotional health means that you are able to keep going regardless of the obstacles that life throws at you. It is impossible to live in a world where everything is perfect, and even with abundance in every area of life, you will experience some setbacks along the way. Emotional well-being is essentially the way you look at and live in wellness. Here, you create in your own life an existence worth having by your own definition. Even if you do not meet the 'universal' definition of wellness, you can still be happy and fulfilled. Emotional wellness helps you in the following ways:

- The first benefit of emotional health is that you identify the meanings behind your emotions. As soon as you do this, you will be in a better position to get to the root cause of any issues. When you do that, you become more proactive instead of being reactive. You develop emotional intelligence, an aspect of emotional well-being that helps us in our dealings with other people.

- Emotional well-being also entails finding out our personal strengths and weaknesses. You then build on the strengths and figure out how to adjust for your weaknesses to reach your highest potential.

- Optimism is also an outcome of emotional wellness. Here, you learn to see the good in the bad and to continue pursuing your goals in spite of the obstacles that you may face.

- You also build a healthy coping mechanism for the difficulties that arise. Whether it is listening to music, going for a run, painting, writing in a diary, or mindful breathing exercises, emotionally adjusted people have that one thing that allows them to cope with stressful situations.

- You discover your interests, hobbies, and leisure activities and pursue them. An interest besides your job, relationship, or family can go a long way in ensuring your emotional health. It is how you unwind and get back in touch with your inner self where your interests take the fore.

- Emotional health also brings out your sense of creativity. Whether it be in your career or in your leisure activities, you will express yourself better creatively when your emotions are well balanced.

- However, at the end of the day, emotional well-being is all about realizing your purpose in life and conducting yourself in accordance with that sense of purpose. This allows you to live a life of constant personal growth.

So, how exactly are you supposed to grow your emotional well-being?

First off, you must take note of upsetting emotions. This means that when negative emotions arise, you will look to their root cause and confront it instead of just lashing out or engaging in self-destructive behavior.

Second, you should be able to catch yourself when you judge yourself harshly. It is not a bad thing to be your own biggest critic. In fact, it helps to be hard on yourself. It is the only way to keep constantly improving yourself. But when the criticism stops being constructive and starts being judgmental, you risk giving free reign to negativity in your life. Turn the self-judgment into a moment of compassion and self-love by appreciating yourself instead.

The third strategy to build your emotional curiosity is by examining your thoughts from a position of honest curiosity. Why does a particular thought pop into your mind at the exact same moment? Curiosity allows you to examine your own emotions and the thoughts that trigger so that you can self-diagnose and be a part of your own growth.

Social Well-being

Humans are social beings and the state of our relationships with those close to us makes an important element of overall health. It is only when we manage to build warm, nurturing relationships and a genuine concern for each other's wellness that we can achieve social wellness. A good support network is important for overall well-being mostly because more friends in your social circle means more people to push you to pursue physical, spiritual, emotional, and mental well-being. According to studies, other advantages of social health also include fewer chances of lifestyle diseases like obesity and high blood pressure (AdvantageCare, 2018). Especially with obesity, the peer pressure you feel to maintain a fit and healthy physic is responsible for this benefit.

Social Health Strategies

The first strategy to improving social health is making new connections and maintaining old ones. You can do this by joining a social activity like cooking classes. An added advantage to making connections is that it makes it easier for you to find romantic partners and find love as well.

The second strategy is working to build healthy relationships from the connections you make. It takes time and lots of work to develop an acquaintance into a friendship, but that work is rewarded over time by the peer support you receive.

The third and final way to foster good social health is to engage in social activities. This one is as much a strategy for fostering a better connection as it is for maintaining it. Whether it is game night or a group outing, getting active makes it easier to forge a strong connection.

Even though technology has been eroding the quality and quantity of face-to-face interactions between friends, it is still the best way to maintain social health. Now this is not to say that social media and other digital forms of interaction are completely useless. But studies have found that live interactions increase social connection by as much as 50% (AdvantageCare, 2018). Social media tends to make people very well connected yet still very lonely at the same time.

Mental Health

Mental health is the biggest challenge to human health in the world today. It encompasses emotional and social well-being and affects our thoughts, actions, and feelings. Emotional and social health is especially important for mental health. They help you manage your feelings and also empower you to deal with challenges that arise in your day-to-day life. When your life is touched by trauma, professional treatment is necessary to maintain mental health. Otherwise, you can maintain a good mental state by reducing the amount of stress you carry from day to day. You see mental health issues arise when you accumulate too much stress in your life.

De-stress

Stress is the leading cause of lifestyle diseases. It has been linked with heart disease because it encourages stress eating and reduces chances of exercising. Many people who drink or smoke also do it in more dangerous levels when they are stressed. Moreover, when stress accumulates and continues unchecked for a long time, it leads to depressions – a more serious mental health issue with serious morbidity.

These high stakes make it very important that you deal with stress proactively rather than reactively. This can be done by tapping into the superconscious. This part of the mind is perfectly balanced and tranquil. Manifesting its serenity in your life will give you the chance to enjoy a stress-free life. This can be done by:

Being Positive

Positivity is very important for attracting the magic of the universe for tranquility. Even the simple act of laughing can have a profound impact on mental (and even physical, to some extent) health.

Meditating

Mindfulness meditation helps you to unwind and achieve greater levels of mental health. It allows you to appreciate the present moment and deal with negative emotions from the past. The enhanced emotional balance that meditation brings also helps to maintain a high level of mental wellness.

Gratitude

The worst effect that stress has on well-being is making you see all the bad things in life and forget about the good. This negativity builds and grows until you feel completely overwhelmed. However, by taking the time out of your day to take stock of your life and be grateful for the good things, you will unleash a wave of positive energy into the universe and attract good feelings and positivity.

Exercising

Exercise doubles as a very potent remedy for stress. It has been proven that exercise helps your body to produce endorphins that boost mood and increase serotonin levels in the brain (Harteneck, 2015). Serotonin is the pleasure hormone, so more of it means more joy in your life and lower stress levels. And while you are at it, spend some time in nature as well. It goes a long way in reducing stress.

Talk to Someone

Your social group is crucial to maintaining good mental health. When you get a listening ear, you start feeling more valued, more positive, and less stressed. Moreover, when you trust someone with what is troubling you, you start to see the positive aspects of other people as well as yourself.

Do Some Good

Helping other people also boosts your mental well-being. The gratitude of other people when you do something nice makes you feel good about yourself, brings meaning to life, and gives you a more positive outlook on life. It also places you in a better position to engage in activities that help you to manifest mental well-being in your life.

Chapter 7: Peace

Peace is a state where you experience mental and emotional serenity. When you are at peace, you don't experience any sort of anxiety or worry. When you have inner peace, you will have the opportunity to enjoy all the abundance you have attracted from the universe. In this chapter, we will discuss the different ways through which you can manifest peace into your life by tapping into the magic of the universe.

Let Go of Perfectionism

The pursuit of perfection is one of the most unsettling things for the mind. It means that you will never really be settled or satisfied with what you have. Every time you reach a new level of success, you immediately embark on pursuing something bigger. Perfectionism also makes it very hard to avoid comparing yourself with others because it makes you feel that success is not enough on its own. You have to be better than everyone. You have to be mistake-free. Yes, mistakes are common even in the pursuit of abundance and you must be willing to make a few before you can reach your highest potential.

Perfectionism also means that you will probably not be satisfied with the things you attract from the universe and will drive yourself harder to get there. This tendency leads to low self-esteem and increases worry, especially when it seems like you will not get what you are looking for.

The fear of failure that is associated with perfectionism and the procrastination that comes with it also present a case of double jeopardy. The double jeopardy is caused by the fact that fear of failure and procrastination leads to poor performance. With the poor performance, you become even more stressed and deliver even less. The fact that you do badly reinforces the belief that you can't do it, and the cycle perpetuates all over again.

Until you realize that perfectionism is a moving target you simply are never going to hit, you will be a person chasing shadows. Instead of being motivated to do better in future by unmet goals, you will be depressed and probably remain so for longer than is strictly healthy. Embrace imperfection and you will overcome the negative emotions associated with failure. Only then will you achieve peace of mind and strengthen your ability to attract a magical destiny from the universe.

Listen to Your Heart

Sometimes it is necessary to make changes to your life to bring about peace of mind. A bad job, for example, can be a serious impediment to well-being and positivity. Until you change it, you won't be able to attract the magic of the universe. It is your job to eliminate anything that you feel does not contribute to your well-being. This can be done by:

Creating a Life Plan

A life plan gives you a sense of purpose and direction in life. Like a lighthouse, it helps you determine the direction you need to take your life at every point of your life. And because decision-making is something that causes doubts and chaos, a life plan ensures that your efforts in making decisions is limited to the execution of a well determined course of action. As long as you are true to yourself when creating the life plan, you will find immense satisfaction in pursuing it.

A good life plan is one that is aligned with the magical destiny that the universe has for every one of us. Make sure that you get in touch with your superconscious mind while you craft a life plan to pursue.

Follow Through on It

A life plan is useless if you don't follow through and realize the magical destiny to which it points you. The way to do this is by starting with small steps and small tasks. The more you do these tasks, the more you will build up towards your magical destiny. Success in every one of these small steps will motivate you to work harder towards your dream life.

Enlist the Help of Friends

Whatever your life plans, chances are that it is really big and almost impossible to achieve on your own. Well, this is actually a good thing. Doing things with friends ensures that you always have a support network to keep you motivated when things go wrong.

Prudent Use of Social Media

Sometimes it is very difficult to be at peace while you are constantly getting bombarded with a barrage of information about other people's "perfect" life. It is very difficult to stop yourself from comparing when there is so much of other people's achievements to check yourself up against. Even when you do something worthwhile, there will always be someone out there who will have done a "better" job. So, instead of celebrating what you have, you will start feeling bad about what you don't.

Another reason to avoid social media is because it amplifies your fear of missing out. The fear of missing out makes it incredibly easy to abandon your current pursuit for the best new thing or waste your energy with needless activities. Whenever you find yourself falling into the trap of comparisons and doing things simply out of the fear of missing out, it is better to disconnect.

Avoid Materialism

This may seem like a contradictory concept in a book about manifesting abundance in every area of your life, but it is an important idea nonetheless. The essence of it is that money and possessions are not the only important things in life. Love, health, happiness, and peace of mind are just as important. Even though shopping for something you have desired for a long time will make you feel good to finally get it, after a while the excitement will wear off. Moreover, materialism encourages needless competition and dissatisfaction. No sooner will you see someone with something you loved having than you will be feeling less fulfillment. Instead of seeking fulfillment from material things, recognize that money is just a means to an end. As long as you have what you need, happiness, love, and peace count for more.

Reconcile with the Past

You can never be at peace with the present if you are still hung up on the past. Being hung up makes it very difficult to remain focused on the present or even to dedicate yourself fully to your future pursuits. There is nothing you can do about the past, so there is no use in even trying. It will just disrupt your peace of mind.

Mistakes are especially disruptive to peace. Because they denied you something for which you had worked really hard, they hurt the worst. However, you must recognize that no amount of regret can change the past. The best strategy to follow is to find out if there is anything you can do. If there is, don't hesitate. If there is nothing to be done, then you must accept and move on.

You have to forgive yourself and others who may have hurt you in the past, otherwise the grudges you hold will destroy your future with bitterness and negativity. Recognize that to err is human and you can learn from your mistakes. This way, you achieve true reconciliation and will be able to move forward in the most productive way possible.

Forgive

Forgiveness heals the soul. Grudges, on the other hand, bring only misery. Even worse, keeping a grudge distracts you from attracting the magic of the universe into your life. If you want to establish a transcendental connection with the universe, you must let go of all feelings of resentment you hold against someone or the world. Even if the world has dealt you a bad hand in the past, letting the feelings of resentment take root in your mind will only end up derailing you even more.

When you forgive, you free up your mind to focus on your blessings rather than the wrongs perpetrated against you. It is a positive outlook that sets you on the path to abundance manifestation right there. Because when you choose to forgive, you make the decision to focus on what is right with the world, not what is wrong with it. Every time you choose to look at the positive side of life in the midst of negativity, you enhance your energy levels and attract the magic of the universe over your life in spectacular fashion.

Remove Media Distractions

The media is the largest treasure trove of turbulence that you can unleash in your life. It has been established that all media, including radio, television, magazines, video games, and entertainment, affect our minds in a negative way. The timing of your media consumption also plays a huge part in this relationship. For example, watching a horror movie before bed will probably bring you nightmares, hard rock music makes people more rebellious, and sometimes the news are extremely depressing. The following strategies will help you block negative influences from the media and maintain a state of peacefulness in your life.

1. Do not watch distressing movies, especially horror and thrillers, before bed. It is definitely harmful to binge watch on Netflix all weekend, so limiting your movie consumption all together would be a great idea too.

2. Limit the amount of time you spend in front of the television to the lowest possible figure. If you feel that you are up to it, you can even quit watching it altogether. You will have succeeded in blocking a huge amount of distressing content from reaching your brain and disrupting your peace of mind. We live in a society that glories in tragedy, so our news pump our lives with sadness and gore as much as possible. From wars in far-off lands to corruption and dirty politics at home, you only get chaos from the media.

3. Listen to uplifting music. It is very tempting to go dark when you are going through a rough patch. The music helps you express the aggression that you can't. The one thing it does not do is help you deal with your issues or rise above them. But when you choose to listen to uplifting music, you fight chaos with positivity, not more chaos.

Fight the Right Battles

Even the best army in the world would lose a war if it just waded into one without regard for the issues. With your limited mental energies, you cannot afford to waste your time fighting with others over every small issue. It is important that you choose the right battles to fight in. This way, you will stand more chances of winning. You will also avoid plunging your life into chaos for something that is of no consequence.

Tolerate People More

At least a very big barrier to peace and tranquility in life is the displeasure we feel when others do things we don't approve of. The more you think about the politicians who oppose efforts towards fighting global warming and the people who elect them to office, the more furious you will become. But your fury will do nothing to solve the issue. Unless you can do something about it, don't let it get to you.

Journal

Writing your experiences in a journal helps you to unleash the thoughts and feelings that create chaos in your mind. Whether you type it out on your computer or you use pen on paper, journaling can bring you immense peace because it lets you unload your burdens without the fear of judgment. By writing them down, you also get the chance to process seemingly complicated situations and figure a way out.

Meditation

And of course, we cannot forget the role that meditation plays in bringing peace and tranquility in life. This practice helps to establish enduring peace of mind by creating a great foundation for it. With meditation, you will manage to calm your mind right down, cope with stress, and ease anxiety in every area of your life.

Simply practicing mindfulness meditation for about twenty minutes every day is enough to accrue the aforementioned benefits. As your mind will get used to settling down for long periods at a time, so will your anxiety and worry levels.

Chapter 8: Inner Happiness

To be happy is the ultimate aim of pretty much everyone on earth. "The pursuit of happiness" is the most enduring principle of the U.S. and the driving force for hundreds of millions of Americans and billions of people all over the world. However, we live in a turbulent world and if you are not careful, it will sap at your happiness until you are left bitter and ravaged.

In the process of manifesting abundance in life, you will encounter numerous challenges and failures. If you don't find the resolve to be happy in spite of these difficulties, your journey could turn ominous pretty quick. In this chapter, we will look at the best strategies to ensure that you live a happy life by finding inner happiness and projecting it to the world even in the worst possible situations.

Keys to Happiness

Inner happiness protects you from the rough and tumble of this world. It makes it possible for you to carry on in a tranquil manner even when all around you are warnings that things might not be too good. Happiness can be achieved by living by a very specific set of rules as discussed in this section.

Envision Your Happiness

Envisioning is the first step in the journey of acquisition. When you see yourself reaching a particular goal in your mind, you get closer to getting it in reality. Regardless of what you wish to get, envisioning precedes receiving. It is this vision that will keep you motivated and happy during those dark moments when it appears like there is no path to fulfillment. When you envision the goal in a realistic manner, with emotions and everything, it is as if you get it first then wait for it to appear in the real world. You will become so convinced that you will receive it in due time that you start feeling the gratitude and the satisfaction beforehand.

Envisioning your goal happening also improves your confidence in your own abilities to reach a specific objective. On the flip side of envisioning is the fear of disappointment, which causes many people to chase their dreams blindly (without envisioning them) and, more often than not, fail at it.

Accept the World as Is

In an ideal world, we would all get all our desires fulfilled with no effort. However, the world is not ideal and we have to strive to get what we want. We have to face off against others who want what we want, against people in power who don't appreciate the things we do, and our own faults and their consequences. But the ideal world is a myth, and you have to deal with the world as it is- imperfect. Even perfection is a shadow that will send you running around in circles and ultimately fill your heart with disappointment and sadness.

Instead of wishing for the ideal or chasing perfection, focus on attaining greatness instead. This is the one thing that anyone who works hard enough and smart enough can get. You will have to work hard, apply yourself to your career or business with everything you got, but you can do this. If you persevere through obstacles and opposition, you will ultimately get there.

Listen to Your Gut

Decisions are a part of our daily life. You make hundreds to thousands of them every day, both in your personal and professional life. And while you might think that a good decision is one that leads to great opportunity and abundance, studies have found that people gauge their decisions based on the feelings it evokes in them. If you make the decision not to invest

Conclusion

The brain is the most powerful organ in the human body. It has the power to connect to the universe and bring us untold prosperity and wealth. The mind is the organ through which we are connected to the universe. So, if you want to attract anything from the universe, you will have to harness the power of the mind. The way we attract things into our lives is through manifesting. When we align our mental, emotional, and physical faculties and transcend the conscious and subconscious mind, we reach a plane of being where limitations are of our own making. Luckily, there are numerous proven strategies to do this. It is these strategies that I have applied myself to explaining within the pages of this book. It is my hope that by reading this book, you will learn some important lessons about life and how to live it – in prosperity.

By far the most important strategy to attract the magic of the universe by harnessing the power of our minds is meditation. It helps us to reach pretty much every goal discussed in this book. Whether your aim is to reach perfect health, inner peace and happiness, or love and friendship, meditation plays a role. The reason why meditation plays such a huge role is because it unlocks the power of the superconscious, the part of the mind that ultimately links us to the infinite source of the universe. In fact, little can be attracted from the universe without activating this part of the mind. Even if you were to combine all other techniques and leave it out, you might still fall short.

In the first chapter, we focused on the magic of the universe and the superconscious mind. It is the magic of the universe that makes it possible for us to manifest abundance in our lives. We can also tap into the magic of the universe to overcome our fears and shift our minds from scarcity to abundance. The superconsciousness plays a part in this by allowing us to discover the purpose of our lives and to develop empathy for others. To reach a state of pure consciousness, you must first quiet the mind, tune into the universe, and synchronize your mind to its vibrations.

Fulfillment in life comes in a big part from having the ability to do what you want when you want to do it. This is why wealth is such an important aspect of abundance. Money gives you the power to travel, enjoy peace and happiness, and to some extent, find love. The most important thing to do to attract money in your life is to develop a magnetic money mindset. You do this by creating a vision, eliminating the things that annoy you from your life, learning to respect money, investing the money you have prudently, working on improving yourself, and practicing gratitude. Gratitude creates positivity, increases energy vibrations, and attracts even more from the universe.

Love is also very important for abundance. With no love, life would be bland and tasteless. The first step to acquiring an abundance of love in your life is to love yourself. In its turn, self-love requires that you examine yourself and understand yourself perfectly, let go of judgments against yourself, and commit to striving for happiness. Only when you do this can you be in the right state of mind to attract love, tap into the inner love flow of the universe, and form deep connections with loved ones in your life.

The way to attract friendship is somewhat similar to attracting love, with the major difference being that you can use friendships to propel yourself ahead in life through mastermind relationships. The concept of mastermind or destiny friendships was first suggested by Napoleon Hill in *Think and Grow Rich* and it has helped some of the world's richest men and women accumulate their vast fortunes. The ultimate secret to manifesting healthy friendships in your life is to work tirelessly on yourself till you get to that place where you are in perfect peace with who you are.

And in every aspect of life, success comes from understanding exactly what you want and then working tirelessly till you get it. However, you must clear the path to this success by eliminating limiting beliefs, clearing mental blocks, and visualizing. You must be careful to avoid getting caught in negative self-fulfilling prophecies about your life, repelling away your success by engaging in the Texas Sharpshooter Fallacy, and engaging in confirmation bias. All these simply hinder your manifestation by deceiving you into believing that you are receiving your wishes even when nothing of the sort is really happening.

Health is an important tenet of abundant living. Good health makes it possible to actually enjoy the prosperity you earn. And for wholesome health, you must ensure that you stay healthy physically, emotionally, spiritually, socially, and mentally. All these areas are interconnected and suffering ill-health in one could easily lead to ill-health in all or most of the other areas. You must therefore ensure that you maintain perfect health through preventative measures and universal healing.

Finally, we discussed peace of mind and happiness. These are important for abundance too, even more so than all other areas discussed in this book. Not only are they crucial on their own, but they also affect the state of the mind and our ability to manifest. Failure to keep them in good levels of abundance means that you will not even be able to manifest money, love, or friendships. To attract inner peace and happiness, you must focus on getting in touch with the inner self, envisioning your vision, letting go of perfectionist tendencies, and tenacity even when failure seems to be imminent.

References

Conlon, J. (2014). *The Magic of the Universe.* Barbados: Crucible Multinational Media Development

Atkinson, W. W. (2012). *The Subconscious and the Superconscious Planes of Mind.* Hollister: YOGeBooks

Huffman, C. (2017). *Poverty Consciousness.* Scotts Valley: CreateSpace Publishing.

Ahmed, I. (2018). Manifest Now. (self published)

Dean, G. (2017). 4 Ways To Shift Your Money Mindset From Scarcity To Abundance. *Forbes.* Retrieved from https://www.forbes.com/sites/gingerdean/2017/12/31/4-ways-to-shift-your-money-mindset-from-scarcity-to-abundance/#83abe2a3a370 on 28th September 2019

McKay, B., & McKay, K. (2010). Iron Sharpens Iron: The Power of Master Mind Groups. *Art of Manliness.* Retrieved from https://www.artofmanliness.com/articles/iron-sharpens-iron-the-power-of-master-mind-groups/ on 28th September 2019

Hurst, K. (n.d.). How To Attract Money And Wealth With The Law Of Attraction. *The Law of Attraction.* Retrieved from http://www.thelawofattraction.com/attract-money-wealth/ on 28th September 2019

Mindworks Team (2019). Top 10 Celebrities who Meditate. *Mindworks*. Retrieved from https://mindworks.org/blog/top-10-celebrities-who-meditate/ on 28th September 2019

AdvantageCare (2018). Social Wellness is the Key to a Healthy Lifestyle. *AdvantageCare Health Centers*. Retrieved from https://advantagecaredtc.org/social-wellness/ on 28th September 2019

Harteneck, P. (2015). 9 Ways You Can Improve Your Mental Health Today. *Psychology Today*. Retrieved from https://www.psychologytoday.com/us/blog/women-s-mental-health-matters/201510/9-ways-you-can-improve-your-mental-health-today on 28th September 2019

·

Made in the USA
San Bernardino, CA
29 January 2020

63784652R00075